GREAT ILLUSTRATED CLASSICS

THE MERRY ADVENTURES OF
ROBIN HOOD

Howard Pyle

**adapted by
Deborah Kestel**

Illustrations by
Pablo Marcos Studio

BARONET BOOKS, New York, New York

GREAT ILLUSTRATED CLASSICS

edited by
Malvina G. Vogel

Contents

About the Author

Howard Pyle was born in Wilmington, Delaware in 1853. After he finished high school, he went to an art school and then worked in his father's leather shop. Soon he returned to the work he loved best—illustrations—and opened his own school for young artists.

Pyle liked to create special worlds where anything could happen. He called them "lands of fantasy or imagination." Sometimes he used his brush to capture these worlds in pictures, and sometimes his pen to write the stories himself. These stories include pirate adventures on the high seas, vivid tales of American colonial life, and legends of knights in the days of chivalry.

In *The Merry Adventures of Robin Hood,* Pyle invites us into one of his fantasy lands. The many tales of Robin Hood come from medieval songs and ballads. They were originally sung to tunes played on a harp, but over the years they became stories. The storytellers of old carried all these tales in their heads.

Howard Pyle gathered these old tales and retold them in his own way, writing them down so anyone could open a book anytime, anyplace, and step into one of the worlds he liked best.

People You Will Read About

Robin Hood, *the bold outlaw of Sherwood Forest*

Will Stutely

Little John

David of Doncaster

Arthur a Bland

Will Scarlet

Allan a Dale

Midge the Miller

Wat the Tinker

} *Robin's Merry Yeoman*

Friar Tuck, *the friar of Fountain Abbey*

Fair Ellen, *the girl Allan a Dale loves*

The Sheriff of Nottingham }

The Bishop of Hereford } *Robin's Enemies*

Guy of Gisborne, *an evil thief and murderer*

Sir Richard of Lea, *a knight*

Sir Henry of Lea, *Sir Richard's son*

King Henry }

Queen Eleanor } *rulers of England*

Richard Partington, *the Queen's page*

King Richard, *Henry's successor as King of England*

The Prioress, *Robin's evil cousin*

Robin Hood and His Merry Band

CHAPTER 1

Robin Hood Becomes an Outlaw

In merry England in olden times, when good King Henry ruled the land, there lived in the green glades of Sherwood Forest, near Nottingham, a famous outlaw named Robin Hood. No archer ever lived who could shoot an arrow with such skill, and there never were such yeomen as his merry band of one hundred fifty men. All the band were outlaws, yet the country people loved them. No one who came to jolly Robin for help ever went away with an empty hand.

But Robin wasn't always an outlaw. This

story will tell how he became one.

When Robin was eighteen, with a strong body and bold heart, the Sheriff of Nottingham proclaimed a shooting match. A large barrel of ale would go to the best shot with a bow and arrow. When Robin heard of the match, he said, "I will go too and draw my string, not only for the barrel of ale, but to win the smile of Maid Marion as well."

The month was May and flowers covered the meadow. Apple buds blossomed, and the cuckoo and lark could be heard in the hedge. The air was sweet, and Robin whistled as he thought of Maid Marion.

As he walked through the forest at dawn, Robin suddenly came upon fifteen of the King's foresters seated beneath a great oak tree. Each man was dressed in bright green, or Lincoln green as it was called. They made a fine show, feasting on meat pie and foaming ale. One of them, with his mouth full,

Robin Comes Upon the King's Foresters.

called out to Robin, "Halloa, where are you going, my lad, with your bow and arrows?"

When Robin told them he was off to Nottingham Town to shoot for the prize, they all laughed aloud. They called him a boasting infant and told him he had no chance of winning.

That made Robin angry, for no lad likes to be teased. He boldly made a bet that he could bring down the best in a herd of deer more than sixty yards away. He took his good strong bow made of yew wood and, placing the tip at his instep, he strung it. He fitted a broad arrow onto the string and raised the bow, drawing back the gray goose feather to his ear. The next moment the bowstring rang, and the arrow sped like a hawk in the wind, killing the deer dead.

"Ha!" cried Robin with his hand on his hip. "How do you like that shot, good fellows?"

All the foresters were filled with rage, for

Aiming at a Herd of Deer

they had lost their bet. Not only that, Robin had killed one of the King's deer that was in their care.

When the foresters did not answer, Robin looked at them grimly, turned on his heel, and strode away. His heart was bitter and angry. They had teased him, made a false bet with him, and cheated him.

Now it would have been well if the fellow who had first spoken had left Robin alone, but he was drunk and angry about the lost bet. Suddenly, and without a warning, he sprang to his feet and sent an arrow whistling after Robin.

The arrow buzzed within three inches of Robin's head. Quickly he turned around and cried, "You said I was no archer, but say so now again!"

Robin sent an arrow in return, and the forester fell with a cry. Before the others could move, Robin had disappeared into the

An Arrow Buzzes by Robin's Head.

forest.

As he ran through the greenwood, all the joy and brightness were gone from Robin's life. His heart was sick with sadness because he had killed a man.

And so he came to live in the forest that was to be his home for many years to come, for he had become an outlaw. The Sheriff of Nottingham swore that he would bring Robin Hood to justice, not only because he wanted the two hundred pounds reward for Robin's capture, but also because the dead forester was related to him.

But Robin Hood stayed hidden in Sherwood Forest for one year, gathering around him many other outlaws like himself. Some were wanted for hunting the King's deer in cold winter when they had no food; some had been taxed so heavily they had no money to live; and some had been turned out of their farms so that their land might be added to

Robin's Heart Is Sick with Sadness.

the King's property in Sherwood Forest. All had come to escape the unfair treatment they had been given at the hands of the King.

During that year, over a hundred strong yeomen gathered about Robin Hood and chose him to be their leader and chief. They missed no chance to take from the rich and proud who had ruined them. To the poor folk, they lent a helping hand and returned the money that had been unjustly taken from them. The people found they had nothing to fear from Robin and his outlaw band, so they began to tell many tales of the merry men of Sherwood Forest. These are the tales that I will tell to you now.

Telling Tales of the Merry Men

Washing in the Cold Brown Brook

CHAPTER 2

Robin Hood Meets Little John

One morning when all the birds were singing among the leaves, Robin and all his men awoke. Each fellow washed his head and hands in the cold brown brook that leaped laughing from stone to stone.

Then Robin announced, "Today I go to seek adventure. Wait here in the greenwood, my merry men. I shall blow three blasts upon my bugle horn if I need you. Then come quickly, for I shall want your aid."

He walked to the edge of Sherwood and wandered for a long time through highway and byway. He met many people—a fair lady, a fat monk, a gallant knight, a plump lass— but he found no adventure.

At last, he came to a narrow bridge made of one log laid across a pebbly stream. There was room enough for only one person to cross. Then he saw a tall stranger coming from the other side. Each man walked faster, thinking to cross first.

"Now stand back," shouted Robin, "and let the better man cross first."

"No!" answered the stranger. "Stand back yourself, for *I* am the better man."

Then Robin and the stranger began to boast to each other. Robin was tall, but the stranger was taller by a head, for he was seven feet tall. The man was also much broader than Robin. Even so, it was not long before Robin challenged him to a bout with staffs on the bridge. The first man to fall would tumble into the water.

Robin Challenges the Tall Stranger.

"I'll gladly wait while you cut a stick to use as a staff," said the stranger, laughing and twirling his own staff till it whistled in the air above his head.

The Knights of King Arthur's Round Table never met in a fiercer fight than these two. Robin and the stranger stood face to face on the bridge for one good hour. Many blows were given and received till here and there were bumps and sore bones on both. Each man marveled at the other's strength. Then the stranger gave Robin a crack on the head. Robin lost his temper and swung with all his might at the stranger. But the man caught him off balance, and Robin fell head over heels into the water.

"And where are you now, good lad?" shouted the stranger, roaring with laughter.

"Oh, floating with the tide," said Robin, laughing at himself. He waded to the bank, frightening and scattering the little fish with

"And Where Are You Now, Good Lad?"

his splashing. Then he clapped his horn to his lips and blew a blast that echoed sweetly down the forest paths.

"I must say you are a sturdy soul and a strong fighter," said Robin.

"And you," said the stranger, laughing, "you take your beating bravely."

Soon the twigs and branches rustled, and suddenly twenty or thirty of Robin's strong yeomen, all dressed in Lincoln green, burst from the forest with Will Stutely leading them.

When they heard that this stranger had given their chief a good dunking, they moved to treat him to the same. But the stranger was so strong, he held them off, and more than one yeoman got a bruised head.

Robin asked the stranger to join his band, and the man replied, "If there is any man here who can shoot a better arrow than I, I might."

The Yeomen Defend Their Leader.

The stranger chose the strongest bow, next to Robin's own, and sent an arrow so straight that it hit the very center of the mark made on an oak tree eighty yards away.

Even Robin's own men clapped enthusiastically at such a fine shot.

"Aha!" cried the stranger. "Do better if you can."

Robin took up his bow and shot with his very greatest skill. The arrow flew straight, and it split the stranger's arrow into splinters. The yeomen leaped to their feet, waved their caps, and cheered.

"That is a shot, indeed!" cried the stranger. "Now I will be one of your men. I am called John Little."

Then Will Stutely, who loved a good joke, spoke up. "No, stranger. I do not like your name, so I will change it. You are so *small* and *frail*, I think I will call you Little John."

With that, Will emptied a pot of ale over

"That Is a Shot, Indeed!"

the stranger's head and christened him Little John, while Robin Hood and all his band laughed aloud. At first, Little John was angry, but he soon found he could not stay angry for long because the others were so merry. So he laughed with the rest. Then Robin clothed him from top to toe in Lincoln green and gave him a good yew bow.

Little John was now a member of Robin Hood's merry band.

Will Stutely Christens Little John.

The Sheriff Writes the Warrant.

CHAPTER 3

The Tinker Joins Robin's Band

The Sheriff of Nottingham had sworn to capture Robin Hood and collect the two hundred pounds reward. But the Sheriff did not know about Robin's band, and he thought he could serve a warrant for his arrest on Robin just as he would on any lawbreaker—with the help of the citizens of the town.

But the men of Nottingham Town knew of Robin and his doings, and many laughed when they thought of anyone handing the bold outlaw a warrant. They knew that all they would get would be cracked heads, so not one of them offered to serve the Sheriff's warrant.

After his failure in Nottingham Town, the Sheriff sent a messenger to Banbury Town. There, the messenger found a shaggy-haired tinker, a metalworker, who thought he could easily capture this rascal, Robin Hood.

One bright morning soon after this, Robin started off to Nottingham to find what was happening there. He walked merrily, and his eyes and thoughts wandered. His bugle horn hung at his hip and his bow and arrows at his back. In his hand he carried an oaken staff, which he twirled with his fingers as he strolled along.

As he strolled down a shady lane, Robin saw a tinker coming. The tinker's bag and his hammer hung on his back. He carried a strong staff and sang in a loud voice.

Robin gave him a saucy greeting, and soon the two were joking and heading to the Blue

The Tinker Walks Along Singing.

Boar Inn for some home-brewed ale.

"Tell me your news, friend," said Robin, "for tinkers are always full of tales."

"I have a task that calls for all my wits. I seek a bold outlaw who men call Robin Hood. In my pouch, I have a warrant with the Sheriff's red seal on it. Do you know this Robin Hood, good fellow?"

"I saw him just this morning," said Robin. "But tinker, men say he is a sly fox. Be careful or he might steal your warrant right from your very pouch."

"He may be sly, but I am sly too," cried the tinker. "What does the man look like, lad?"

"Much like me," said Robin, "my age, height and build. He has blue eyes like mine too." And Robin winked at him.

"I thought he was a great bearded man," said the tinker.

"Not so large," said Robin, "but men say he's a right good fighter."

"Tinkers Are Always Full of Tales."

With this, they entered the Blue Boar Inn. No sweeter inn could be found—shaded and cool in the summer, cozy and full of good company in the winter. The inn was well-known to Robin and his band. He and Little John or Will Stutely or young David of Doncaster often gathered there when the forest was filled with snow.

The innkeeper knew when to keep quiet, and when Robin and the tinker entered, he made no sign to give Robin away. Robin made sure the tinker drank deeply, while he only wet his lips. First the man sang, then his head began wagging, until at last he fell asleep. Then Robin laughed aloud and quickly took the warrant from the tinker and disappeared.

The next day, at a sudden bend in the road, Robin and the tinker met sharply face to face.

"Halloa, my sweet bird," said Robin.

Robin Steals the Warrant.

The tinker was grim. Not only had he been left to pay the bill for the ale, but he now knew that it was Robin Hood himself who had tricked him. He spat upon his hands and came at Robin with his staff.

Robin was quick and moved like a cat, but his staff broke under the tinker's mighty blows. Robin reached for his horn and blew three blasts, loud and clear.

"Blow if you will," said the tinker, "but you will go to the Sheriff with me."

Then Little John and six burly yeomen in Lincoln green leaped out of the forest.

"Why do you blow your horn so loudly, good master?" cried Little John.

"This tinker," said Robin, "would like to take me to Nottingham to hang."

"He shall hang!" cried Little John, and he began to tie the tinker's hands with his bowstring.

"No," said Robin, holding Little John's

The Tinker's Mighty Blow!

arm, "he is a good man and brave too. And he sings a lovely ballad." Robin looked at the tinker and asked, "Will you join my men? You shall have three suits of Lincoln green and forty marks a year."

The tinker agreed to the merry life, and they all headed back into the forest depths, where the tinker was to live forever, singing ballads to Robin's band.

Robin Stops Little John.

The Sheriff Makes Plans.

CHAPTER 4

The Nottingham Shooting Match

Now the Sheriff was very angry when his plan failed. He swore he would hang the tinker as a traitor if he ever caught him. He spoke to no one and no one spoke to him, for he spent all his time alone, thinking of a plan to take Robin. Finally, he found one that couldn't fail.

He decided to proclaim a great shooting match and offer a prize so grand that daring Robin would risk a day among the Sheriff's men to show his skill. The Sheriff planned to surround him before he could escape.

So, the Sheriff sent messengers north and south, east and west, announcing the match. The prize was to be an arrow of pure gold.

Robin Hood first heard the news in Lincoln Town. He hurried back to Sherwood and called to his men, "Our friend the Sheriff has proclaimed a shooting match. I would like one of us to win the golden arrow. What do you say, lads?"

Young David of Doncaster spoke, "I have come from our friend Eadom of the Blue Boar Inn. He tells me that this knavish Sheriff is laying a trap for you at this shooting match. So do not go, good master, for I know he seeks to harm you."

"Now," said Robin, "you just keep your ears open and your mouth shut, as a wise and crafty woodsman should. No, good David, we shall not be afraid of the Sheriff. We will meet his tricks with our own tricks. Some of us will dress as friars, some as tinkers, and

David of Doncaster Warns Robin.

some as beggars. I will go too and shoot for this golden arrow, and if I win it, we will hang it in our greenwood tree."

The day of the Nottingham shooting match was a colorful jumble of ribbons, flower garlands, silk banners, bells, ale, tents, and food carts. Every seat on the benches surrounding the shooting range was taken.

The Sheriff leaned forward in his place and looked keenly among the archers for Robin Hood. But there was no one dressed in the Lincoln green that he and his band wore.

After the first two rounds, only three of all the strong and famous archers gathered that day were left. One was Gill o' the Red Cap, one Adam o' the Dell, and one—a tattered stranger in scarlet with a patch over one eye. Of these men, only the stranger was near Robin Hood's height and build. But his hair and beard were brown, not yellow as Robin's, and he was blind in one eye.

The Day of the Shooting Match

The people laughed when the tattered stranger stepped forward to shoot, for they thought no man could aim with only one eye. They were silenced when his arrow flew so true, it hit the target's center.

"What is your name?" asked the Sheriff, as he came down to award the golden arrow.

"Men call me Jock o' Teviotdale," said the stranger.

"I believe that you draw a better bow than that coward, Robin Hood, who dared not come today. Will you join my service?"

"No!" said the man to the Sheriff. "No man is my master."

It was a strange company that gathered around the greenwood tree in Sherwood that day. Among tinkers, friars, beggars, and farmers, there sat one man in tattered scarlet with a patch over one eye. In his hand he held a golden arrow. As the others talked and laughed, he stripped away the patch and

Robin Wins the Golden Arrow.

the rags and showed himself all clothed in Lincoln green.

"These clothes come off easily," he said, "but this walnut stain will stay in my yellow hair a while." For it was Robin himself who had taken the prize from the Sheriff's own hands.

After a feast, Robin took Little John aside and said, "I do not like the Sheriff thinking I am a coward."

Little John winked at Robin and said, "Will Stutely and I will soon send that fat Sheriff news he does not expect."

The Sheriff's dinner in the great hall of his castle was interrupted by a blunted arrow that suddenly flew into the room and landed among the dishes on the table. Tied around the shaft of the arrow was a fine scroll. One of the Sheriff's men pulled the arrow out of the table, unrolled the scroll, and read:

Robin Has Fooled the Sheriff.

"NOW HEAVEN BLESS THY GRACE THIS DAY, SAY ALL THE MEN IN SHERWOOD, FOR YOU JUST GAVE THE PRIZE AWAY TO MERRY ROBIN HOOD."

"Where did this come from?" cried the Sheriff angrily.

"Through the window, your grace," said the man who had taken the arrow from the table.

A Message from Robin Hood

The Sheriff's Men Hunt Robin.

CHAPTER 5

A Daring Rescue

When the Sheriff failed to take Robin by law and tricks, he tried might. He ordered three hundred men to Sherwood Forest to capture the outlaw dead or alive for a reward of one hundred pounds of silver.

When Robin heard of the Sheriff's plan, he said, "Force brings blood. I killed a man once, and I do not wish to kill a man again."

So his band stayed hidden in the depths of the forest for seven days. And for seven days, the Sheriff's men hunted through the forest glades, but did not see one man in Lincoln green.

Early in the morning of the eighth day, Robin said to his men, "Now who will go and find where the Sheriff's men are by this time?"

Every man leaped at the chance, but Robin chose Will Stutely, saying he was the slyest old fox in Sherwood.

Will dressed himself in a friar's robe and hid a great sword beneath it. As he set off for the Blue Boar Inn, he said to himself, "Good Eadom will tell me all the news."

At the Sign of the Blue Boar, he found a band of the Sheriff's men drinking noisily. Without a word to anyone, for he feared his voice might be recognized, he sat down in a corner and waited to speak to the innkeeper alone. As he sat, a large house cat rubbed against his knee, raising his robe a bit. Stutely quickly pushed his robe down again, but one of the Sheriff's men had already seen

Will Stutely Spies on the Sheriff's Men.

the Lincoln green beneath his robe.

Meanwhile, Robin Hood was standing under the greenwood tree thinking of Will Stutely and how he might be, when he saw two of his men running down the path with Maken, the innkeeper's daughter.

"Will Stutely has been captured!" she cried. "And I fear he is hurt badly. They say he will hang in Nottingham tomorrow."

"He shall not!" cried Robin, and he blew three loud blasts on his horn. "Tomorrow I will bring Will Stutely back, or I will die with him." And all the band agreed.

Next day, they all made their way from Sherwood by separate paths to meet in a dell outside Nottingham. Robin sent young David of Doncaster to learn the place and hour set for the hanging. Then he called the band around him and said, "We go straight to town and mix with the people there. Keep one another in sight. Strike no man without

The Innkeeper's Daughter Brings News.

need, but if you do strike, strike hard. Then keep all together till we get back to Sherwood. Let no man leave his fellows."

There was a bustle in Nottingham, and crowds filled the streets knowing that the famous Will Stutely was to be hanged. In the midst of the Sheriff's guard, tied in a cart, rode Will. His face was pale and his hair was matted with blood from his wounds. He looked up and down the crowds as he passed. Some faces showed pity and some, friendliness. But when he saw no one that he knew, his face sank. He remembered the forest, the wild deer, and the laughter of his friends. He looked upon death as a sad thing, and he bowed his head.

Then came a bustle and a noise, and a man tried to push between the guards to reach the cart. When Stutely saw that it was Little John, his heart leaped, for Robin's band was on every side of him.

On the Way to Be Hanged!

Little John struck a guard full on the head and leaped into the cart. "You shall not leave us without saying good-bye, Will," he said, cutting Will's bonds.

Swords flashed in the setting sun, and a score of arrows whistled through the air. The Sheriff rode down on Little John, but he ducked quickly, and the blow passed harmlessly over his head. Robin Hood and his band pushed the guards back, sending a stream of arrows after them as they ran.

"Stay!" shouted Will to the Sheriff. "You will never catch bold Robin Hood if you don't meet him face to face."

Then Will Stutely turned to Little John and tears ran from his eyes. "My own true friend, I thought I would see you next in Heaven," he cried.

Little John could not answer; he was weeping also.

Then Robin Hood gathered his band

Little John Rescues Will.

together with Will Stutely in their midst, and they moved slowly away toward Sherwood. But they left ten of the Sheriff's men lying on the ground wounded.

Thus the Sheriff tried three times to take Robin Hood and failed three times: his warrant failed, his trap failed, and his army in Sherwood failed. This last time frightened him, for he came near to losing his own life. So he stayed inside his castle for many days, ashamed of what had happened in Sherwood that day.

Leaving the Sheriff's Men Wounded

Robin Makes a Deal with the Butcher.

CHAPTER 6

Robin Hood's Revenge

The band lived quietly in the forest for nearly a year, shooting, wrestling, and singing merrily. In that time Robin often thought of ways to even his score with the Sheriff. One day, he got so impatient that he decided to go to Nottingham to see what adventure he could stir up.

On the way, he met a butcher heading for the Nottingham market. Robin had a fancy to enter the town in disguise, so he bought the man's cart, horse, clothes, and all his meat for six marks.

In the market, he set up his stall and sold all his meat at a low price. When a widow or a poor woman came to him, he asked for no money. When a merry lass came, he asked only a kiss.

None of the other butchers sold a penny's worth of meat. Some were angry, but most thought Robin was a jolly lad who had come into much money and wanted to live merrily until it ran out.

"Come, brother," said one of the butchers. "This day, the sheriff has asked all the members of the Butcher Guild to feast with him."

Robin was delighted and immediately agreed.

At the Guild Hall, the Sheriff called Robin to sit by him, not recognizing him in his butcher's dress. The Sheriff had heard that the jolly lad was rich and free with his money. Since he was greedy for money, the

The Busiest Butcher in Nottingham

Sheriff hoped to get some of Robin's into his own pocket.

As dinner was served, the Sheriff asked Robin to say grace. Robin stood and said, "Now Heaven bless us all and this food, and may all butchers be as honest as I." At this, all laughed and clapped.

During the meal, Robin teased the Sheriff and made jokes, laughing all the time. The Sheriff wanted to know how rich this bold fellow was.

"My brothers and I have more than five hundred deer, but we have not been able to sell any of them," answered Robin.

Hearing this, the Sheriff's eyes twinkled, and he offered Robin three hundred pounds for them. Many of the butchers grumbled, saying it was a mean trick to cheat a poor youth, for the deer were well worth seven hundred pounds.

But Robin had a plan. He accepted the

Robin Stands to Say Grace.

three hundred pounds and arranged to take the Sheriff to see the herd that very day.

As the two neared Sherwood, the Sheriff grew worried. He feared the outlaw band.

Robin laughed. "Do not worry," he said, "for I know Robin Hood well, and you should worry about him only as much as you worry about me."

Deeper in the forest shades, they crossed the path of a herd of grayish-brown deer. The Sheriff nodded his head and moved to go, for he was very uneasy, but Robin caught his bridle rein.

"Stay!" said Robin. "You have not met my brothers. They own these deer also." He blew three clear notes, and soon Little John came with one hundred strong fellows.

"Take this bridle, Little John," cried Robin, "for the Sheriff has come to feast with us today."

The Sheriff despaired, for he knew how the

The Sheriff Is Uneasy in Sherwood.

band feasted with rich men. Food and ale flowed merrily, and then the men emptied their guest's purse. And the Sheriff's purse held three hundred pounds.

He wasn't any more pleased when he was led to an oak tree where the feast was laid out, for there hung the golden arrow Robin had won.

Soon, though, the Sheriff was eating and heartily cheering the men as they competed at games with staffs and bows and arrows. At one point, he did not know he was cheering for the very same tinker he had sworn to hang.

The time passed so merrily that the Sheriff thought Robin had forgotten his purse. But no, for when the sun was low and the moon glimmered in the trees, Robin sent Little John to count out the money. Then he thanked the Sheriff and sent him on his way.

"Farewell, sir," said Robin, "and if you ever

Cheering the Games

plan to cheat some poor fellow again, remember your feast in Sherwood."

Then the Sheriff bitterly regretted the day he first mixed with Robin Hood. He thought he could cheat another man, but instead, he cheated himself. For it is true that many men are ruined by their own greed.

"Remember Your Feast in Sherwood."

Harvest Time in October

CHAPTER 7

The Nottingham Town Fair

Spring and summer had long passed, and the mellow month of October had come. Apples had ripened, harvests were gathered, and the air was cool and fresh. It was time for the great fair which was held every five years at Nottingham Town.

Archery had always been the main sport, but this year the Sheriff hesitated to proclaim it, fearing that Robin Hood and his band might come. At last, he decided to offer a prize they wouldn't want—two fat steers.

Little John, Will Stutely, and young David of Doncaster had heard the news at the Blue

Boar Inn. Little John told Robin he wanted to go and shoot, but Robin had some doubts.

"You are my right-hand man and a strong fellow, Little John," said Robin, "even if you are not as cunning as Will Stutely. I could not bear to lose you."

"I will wear scarlet and hide my brown hair in a hood, and no one will know me," said Little John.

So he clad himself in scarlet and set off to the fair. Many people on the road turned to look at the strong, tall fellow in scarlet, and he smiled and nodded back to them.

First he went to the drinking booth where beer and ale flowed and called to all around him to be merry and have a drink with him. Then he went to the dancing booth where three men made sweet music with bagpipes. Here, he laid down his bow and arrows and leaped high, snapping his fingers and charming the lasses with his dancing steps.

Little John Dances at the Fair.

After he had danced a long time, he strolled to the platform where men battled with staffs. Now, Little John loved a good bout, and what happened next is still sung about in ballads to this day.

There was one fellow, Eric o' Lincoln, who cracked the head of every man that met him in the ring. He stood to one side of the ring, boasting of his skill. When he spotted Little John, he called him a long-legged coward. Little John was tired of the man's boasting and wanted to teach him a lesson.

"Is there a man here that will lend me a good strong staff so I may try this fellow?" called Little John.

At this, ten men offered their staffs, and Little John picked the heaviest one. He tossed it up onto the platform, leaped lightly after it, and snatched it up in his hand again.

Those that stood around saw the bravest display of fighting with a staff ever seen in

Eric o' Lincoln Challenges Little John.

Nottingham. Little John and Eric o' Lincoln bouted three full rounds, both guarding themselves so well that no blow was struck till the third round. Then Little John rapped Eric's head. Before Eric could get his balance, Little John swung a blow so heavy, Eric fell as though he would never move again. This ended the famous bout.

But now, the time had come for the long-bow match, and a crowd followed Little John to the range. Though every man shot well, Little John was the best of all, and the crowd cheered him.

"Horrah for Reynold Greenleaf!" they cried, for this was the name Little John had called himself that day.

Then the Sheriff stepped down from his raised seat and came to where the archers stood. He looked closely at Little John and said, "I think I have seen your face before."

"Perhaps," said Little John, "for I have

Congratulating Little John

often seen Your Worship." But the Sheriff did not suspect who he was.

"Reynold Greenleaf," said the Sheriff, "you are the best hand at the longbow I have ever seen, next to that knave Robin Hood. Would you join my service, good fellow? You would have good pay, three suits of clothes a year, and good food and ale."

Little John agreed to this, for he thought he might find some merry jokes if he worked in the Sheriff's house.

To celebrate his victory, Little John gave the steer he had won to the people around him. They built large fires and roasted the steers and drank ale. When the day faded and the moon rose over the spires and towers of Nottingham Town, the people joined hands and danced. Around the fires they went, skipping to the music of bagpipes and harps.

By this time, the Sheriff and his new servant, Reynold Greenleaf, were in the Castle of Nottingham.

"Would You Join My Service?"

An Easy Life for Little John

CHAPTER 8

Life at the Sheriff 's Castle

Little John first entered the Sheriff's service as a joke, but the fireplace was warm in winter, and he was the Sheriff's right-hand man at the table and at hunting. So he put off from day to day going back to Sherwood until six long months had passed and until he had grown as fat as an ox. Then, one day when the Sheriff went hunting, something happened which disrupted Little John's life.

That morning, the Sheriff looked about for Reynold Greenleaf. He wanted to show his noble friends the skill of his man. But Little John lay in bed, snoring till the sun was high in the sky. At last he opened his eyes, but did not move to rise. He lay still, smelling the first days of spring, thinking how sweet everything was this fair morning.

Just then he heard, faint and far away, a distant bugle note sounding thin and clear. He suddenly thought of Robin and Will Stutely, whom he loved better than anyone, and of young David of Doncaster, whom he had trained so well in all sports. A great and bitter longing for them all came over him so, that his eyes filled with tears.

"I will go back to my dear friends and never leave them till life leaves my lips," he cried, leaping from bed.

When he came downstairs, he saw the steward, a large, fat man, standing near the pantry door with a huge bundle of keys. Now the steward hated Little John because the Sheriff liked him so well, so he locked the pantry and refused to give Little John

Little John Longs For His Friends.

anything to eat. He grabbed Little John from behind and began to beat him with the keys.

Little John threw the steward to the floor, broke open the pantry door, and began to eat his breakfast in peace. Now, the cook in the kitchen across the courtyard heard the loud talking and saw Little John throw the steward down. He came running over with an iron bar in his hands.

The steward talked the cook into fighting for him, saying he would pay him ten shillings to teach Little John a lesson. When the cook agreed, the steward crawled away, expecting a might sword fight to begin.

But no, for Little John called, "Hold, good cook, a mighty feast is here. I think we should enjoy it before we fight. What do you say?"

The cook stopped a moment and thought. He loved good feasting, so he agreed.

Both men laid down their swords and sat

The Steward Attacks Little John.

down to a large meat pie. They sat for a long time, eating and singing. After several merry hours had passed, the cook said, "It is late. I have my cooking to do before the Sheriff returns. Let us go and settle this brave fight."

Without waiting, they drew their swords again. Sparks flew at each blow. They fought up and down the hall for an hour or more. Each thought the other a brave swordsman.

At last, Little John cried, "Stop! You are the very best swordsman I ever met. Would you go with me to Sherwood and join with Robin Hood's band? For I am Little John."

The cook seemed lost in amazement. Then he said, "I will go with you, and gladly."

So off they went, plunging into the woods until they came to the greenwood tree where Robin Hood and sixty men sat on the fresh green grass.

Robin and his men leaped to their feet. "Welcome, Little John, welcome!" cried

Two Brave Swordsmen

Robin. "It has been a long time since we heard from you, though we all knew you lived in the castle."

Then Little John told his tale, starting with an account of his bout with Eric o' Lincoln. The men shouted with laughter when their new cook was introduced, but Robin was quiet when Little John and the cook showed him the Sheriff's silver they had brought along. Finally, Robin spoke. "The Sheriff had been punished enough. There was no need to steal his plates too."

Hearing this, Little John jumped up and ran the five miles to where the Sheriff and his company were hunting. He told the Sheriff a strange tale of deer dresed in green and convinced him to come alone into the forest.

When the Sheriff reached the greenwood tree, he looked hard at Little John and suddenly recognized him. "Beware, Little John,"

The Sheriff Recognizes Little John.

he cried, "for you have betrayed me."

"Everything happened today because your steward starved me," said Little John.

The Sheriff saw his cook and his silver and realizing he had been tricked, he bowed his head.

Robin watched him closely for several minutes. "Come, man," he finally said. "I will lead you to your party. I mean to take nothing from you today, for you came here seeking to do no harm."

Then, slinging the bag of silver upon his shoulder, Robin turned away. The Sheriff followed him, too confused to speak. They went forward until they came within a half-mile of the spot where the Sheriff's companions waited.

"Test your servants well from now on, good Sheriff," said Robin. And turning, he left the bewildered Sheriff standing with the sack of money in his hands.

Robin Leaves the Bewildered Sheriff.

A Lazy Day at the Greenwood Tree

CHAPTER 9

The Tanner of Blyth

It was May, and the day was warm and humid. Most of the band were scattered through the forest on one mission or another. A few men lay lazily in the shade of the greenwood tree with Robin. There was great Little John, with limbs as tough as an oak; there was Will Stutely, whose face was brown as a berry from the sun and wind; there was Will Scathelock, who ran as swiftly as a deer; and there was young David of Doncaster, who was almost the size of Little John, although his beard was only fuzz.

Suddenly Robin hit his knee. "We have no Lincoln green cloth in our storeroom," he cried. "Move yourself, Little John! Go straight to Hugh Longshanks of Ancaster and tell him to send us four hundred yards of cloth. Perhaps the journey will take some of the fat of lazy living at our dear Sheriff's off your bones."

"I am not that fat that I could not still hold my footing on a narrow bridge against any yeoman," replied Little John. At this, everyone laughed, for they all remembered the tale of how Robin and Little John had met.

Robin then left them and entered the forest. He stopped at a huge rock which had a room cut into it and a locked oaken door closing it off. This room was the hiding place for the band's money.

Robin took out a bag of gold and gave it to Little John who strapped it onto his broad belt. Then Little John took his seven-foot

The Hiding Place for the Band's Money

staff in his hand and set forth into the forest. He took the leafy path that led to Fosse Way until he came to where the path branched. Here, Little John stopped and rested his chin on his staff. One path led to Ancaster and duty, and the other to the Blue Boar. He chose the Blue Boar, thinking he would rise early the next day and make up for lost time.

Now Arthur a Bland, the tanner, or leatherworker, of Blyth, was passing through Notingham on his way home. He was a champion wrestler. He also had a taste for deer, and though he had no bow, he crept through the underbrush, hoping to spot a herd through the leaves.

When Little John heard the leaves around him rustling, he thought it must be some knave after free deer meat. He stepped forward, challenging Arthur a Bland to a fight with the staff. They attacked each other with

Duty or the Blue Boar Inn?

loud cries.

News had reached Robin that Little John was heading towards the inn instead of going straight to Ancaster. Angered by this, Robin set forth at dawn to seek Little John and tell him how he felt.

Suddenly Robin stopped along the path and listened. "That is Little John's voice and he sounds angry," he said. Robin feared that Little John had been attacked by the King's rangers. He forgot his own anger as he moved quickly through the thicket toward the voices.

In a clearing he saw the tanner and Little John fighting like two great bulls. Little John was the slower, for he was rusty from his stay at the Sheriff's house. If Little John had had his strength, it would have been all over for strong Arthur. But as it was, Arthur dealt a blow that put Little John flat on the ground and sent his staff flying from his

Fighting Like Two Great Bulls

hand as he fell.

"I did not think there was a man in all Nottinghamshire who could do to me what you have done," said Little John from the ground.

"I, too," cried Robin, bursting from the thicket and shouting with laughter, "O man, O man! You went over like a bottle knocked from a wall. This fellow tumbled you over with a pretty rap as I have never seen one tumbled before." Next, turning to the tanner, Robin asked, "What is your name, good fellow?"

"Men call me Arthur a Bland."

"Ha! I have heard your name before. You beat a friend of mine at the Ely Fair last October. The townspeople call him Jock o' Nottingham; we call him Will Scathelock. This poor fellow you knocked to the ground is considered the best fighter with a staff in all England. His name is Little John, and I am

Robin Laughs at Little John's Fall.

Robin Hood."

Little John rose slowly as if his bones had been made of glass. He heard Robin ask Arthur to join his band. Arthur accepted joyfully with a snap of his fingers. He swore there would not be one deer in all Sherwood that would not know the twang of his bowstring.

"As for you, Little John," said Robin, "you will start again for Ancaster, but we will go part way with you, for there are other inns that you know nearby."

Robin Invites Arthur to Join His Band.

Robin Keeps His Eyes on the Road.

CHAPTER 10

Will Scarlet

The three traveled along the sunny road. Robin and Little John cleared up the matter of the Blue Boar between them.

After some distance, the day being warm and the road dusty, they grew thirsty. Just beyond the hedge they found a creek, cold as ice. Kneeling and making cups of their hands, they drank their fill and then stretched their limbs and rested.

Before them, the dusty road ran across a plain. Robin kept his eyes on the road while the other two daydreamed. Suddenly, he pointed and broke the silence. "Look at that gaily-feathered bird."

The others looked and saw a young man walking slowly down the highway. Gaily colored he was indeed, dressed in scarlet silk and velvet, with a broad feather in his cap and threads of gold in his leather scabbard. His hair was long and yellow and curled upon his shoulders.

"By my life!" cried Robin, "I believe he would faint if a furious mouse crossed his path."

Arthur a Bland looked closely at the man and said, "But see how he holds his arms. I swear there are no weak limbs in those fine clothes, only tough muscles."

"I think you are right, friend Arthur," said Little John.

"Pah!" said Robin. "I shall find out who he is. You two stay hidden while I go question the stranger." He stepped forth from the

A Gaily-Feathered Bird

shade of the beech tree and stood in the middle of the road with his hands on his hips.

At first, the man ignored him and tried to walk by him. When Robin refused to allow him to pass and demanded to see his purse, the stranger said sadly and gently, "Good friend, let me continue on in peace, or I fear I must kill you." As he said this, he drew his sword.

"Your sword cannot hold against my oaken staff," said Robin. "Over there is an oaken thicket. Make yourself a good staff."

First the stranger eyed Robin and then his staff. He threw aside the rose he had been carrying all this time, thrust his sword back into the scabbard, and stepped to the roadside. He found a sapling to his liking. He did not cut it, but rolled up his sleeves, placed his heel against the ground, and plucked the young tree up by the roots with one mighty pull.

One Mighty Pull!

When Little John and the tanner saw this, they whistled low under their breath. Whatever Robin thought, he stood his ground. Now he and the stranger in scarlet stood face to face.

This way and that they fought, Robin's skill against the stranger's strength. The dust of the road rose like a cloud. The stranger beat down Robin's guard and laid him lower in the dust than he had ever fallen before.

"Hold!" cried Robin Hood. "I yield."

"Hold!" cried Little John, running from cover with the tanner at his heels.

Robin lay in the road, leaning on his elbows, shaking his head. Little John could not help laughing at poor Robin who was so sore and embarrassed that he angrily pushed away Little John's helping hand.

"What is your name?" Robin asked the stranger.

Watching Skill Against Strength

"My name is Gamwell," came the answer. "I came to find my mother's young brother who men call...."

"Will Gamwell! Don't you know me, lad?" cried Robin, placing both hands upon the young man's shoulders. "Look at me well."

"I do believe you are my Uncle Robin!" he cried, flinging his arms around Robin and kissing him upon the cheek.

"I left you eight or ten years ago," said Robbin, "but I certainly trained you well. I tell you, lad, you are the strongest man I've ever seen. But tell me, why have you left Sir Edward and your mother?"

"It is a sad story, Uncle," said young Gamwell. "You know my father is an easy man and very slow to anger. His steward, a saucy rascal, was always speaking rudely to him. One day I couldn't stand it any longer, so I gave the steward a slap on the ear. And would you believe it—the fellow died! They

"Don't You Know Me, Lad?"

say I broke his neck. So they sent me away to escape the law."

"I am certainly glad to see you, Will, but a man escaping the law doesn't trip daintily along the highway sniffing a rose," said Robin. "We must change your name, for warrants will be out against you. So because of your colorful clothes, you shall be called Will Scarlet."

"I am glad to welcome you among us, Will Scarlet," said Little John, stepping forward and offering his great palm. "I am called Little John, and this is Arthur a Bland who has just joined us."

Then Robin and Little John vowed that no one but the four of them would know of the sound beatings they had taken that day.

"Come. You shall go to Ancaster another time, Little John," said Robin.

So, turning their backs, they retraced their steps back to Sherwood.

Retracing Their Steps to Sherwood

A Meal for Six Pennies

CHAPTER 11

Midge, the Miller' Son

When the four men had been traveling for a long time toward Sherwood and high noon had passed, they began to get hungry. Little John gave Arthur a Bland six pennies and sent him into a nearby inn, while he and the others stepped into the thicket to wait for the tanner's return.

After a time, he came back with a large loaf of brown bread, a fresh round cheese, and a goatskin full of March beer. It was divided into four portions, and the men silently began to eat.

At last, Will Scarlet looked at a small piece

of bread he still held in his hand and said, "I think I will give this to the sparrows." So he threw it from him and brushed the crumbs from his jerkin.

The others had finished also and, taking a last long swallow of the beer, they turned to song.

Robin thought Will Scarlet's song too light for such a strong fellow. Arthur a Bland had to be coaxed to sing, for he was shy. Little John sang next, after much encouragement from the other three, and was only halfway through his song when Robin interrupted him.

"Who is this fellow coming along the road? No, Little John, don't be angry. I have been watching him since you began your song. Look, I pray, and see if you know him."

Little John looked where Robin pointed. "He is a young miller I've seen around the edge of Sherwood," explained Little John.

A Miller Comes Along the Road.

"He surely is no one to spoil a good song about."

"A strong fellow too," said Robin. "I saw him crack Ned o' Bradford's head open quite neatly about two weeks ago."

The young miller was closer now. His clothes were dusted with flour, and over his back he carried a great sack of meal and a thick staff. His cheeks were ruddy, his hair light yellow, and he had just the beginnings of a beard on his chin.

"Let us have some fun with him and pretend we are thieves," said Robin. "Then we will take him into the forest for a merry feast and send him home with gold crowns instead of the pennies he has. What do you say, lads?"

All agreed but Little John, who had no desire to fight and be beaten again that day. Nevertheless, all four men met the miller on the road and immediately surrounded him.

Surrounding the Miller

"What do you want with me?" cried the miller. "You are on Robin Hood's ground, and if he finds you robbing an honest craftsman, he will clip your ears to your head."

"I fear Robin Hood no more than I fear myself," said jolly Robin. "We are four good Christian men who would like to help you carry part of your heavy load."

Slowly and unwillingly the miller untied the mouth of the bag as if to give them the money hidden there. The others gathered round while he thrust his hands in the barley flour. They wondered what he could have inside the bag.

Suddenly he flung handfuls of flour into their faces, filling their eyes, noses, and mouths with it, blinding and half-choking them. While all four stumbled about coughing and rubbing their eyes, the miller tossed another handful and another, until their hair and beards and clothes were as white as

Handfuls of Flour!

snow. Then thwack! thwack! went the miller's staff on their backs.

At last Robin found his horn and clapped it to his lips.

Will Stutely and young David of Doncaster were nearby with a party of Robin's men. When they heard the three blasts, they dashed forward. But what a sight they saw— five white men standing on a white road!

That night, all was ablaze with crackling fires and feasting in the woodlands to welcome the new members to the band, for Midge, the miller's son, had also joined the band and come with them to Sherwood.

Robin stood before the fire and announced, "Today I have gained the three strongest yeomen in all Nottinghamshire and many a sore and bruised bone."

The forest rang with jesting and laughter until at last each man lay down. Then silence fell on all things, and all things seemed to sleep.

Silence Falls on Sherwood.

Planning New Adventures

CHAPTER 12

Allan a Dale

Two day had passed. The morning was bright and the dew still lay on the grass. Robin Hood sat under the greenwood tree. On one side lay Will Scarlet, gazing up into the sky with his hands behind his head. On the other side sat Little John, making a new staff out of a branch. Many others of the band sat or lay nearby.

Robin spoke first. "No one has dined with us for a long time. Therefore our purse is low. Good Stutely, choose six men and go to Fosse Way. Bring someone with a heavy purse to eat with us. We will prepare a grand feast. Take Will Scarlet with you, for he should learn the ways of the forest."

"I choose Midge the Miller and Arthur a Bland also," said Will, "for they are tough fighters with a staff. Is it not so, Little John?"

Everyone laughed except Little John and Robin, who said, "I can speak for Midge and my cousin Scarlet. This very morning, I looked at my ribs, and they are all shades of purple and blue."

Will Stutely and his band set forth to Fosse Way. Many travelers passed there, unaware of the seven strong fellows who lay hidden in the thicket. But no rich esquire, tax man, or fat abbot came by—no one whose purse might be emptied. The band waited the entire day.

"What bad luck!" said Stutely. "Come lads, let us return." So they all turned their toes back to Sherwood.

Waiting for a Purse to Be Emptied

After a time, Will Stutely, who was in the lead, stopped. "Listen, lads!" he whispered. "I think I hear a sound, for truly I have ears like a fox." Then they all heard a faint and melancholy sound, like someone weeping.

"Someone may need our help," said Will Scarlet. He walked towards the sound.

In a clearing in the woodland, they found a pool. By the side of the pool beneath a willow stood a youth weeping aloud. His golden curls were tangled and his clothes were wrinkled. He looked full of sorrow and woe. Over his head in the branches of the willow hung a beautiful harp of polished wood inlaid with gold and silver. Beside him lay an ashen bow and ten fine, smooth arrows.

"Halloa!" shouted Will Stutely. "Who are you, lad, and why are you standing here killing all the green grass with the salt water of your tears?"

Hearing the voice, the lad sprang to his

A Weeping Youth

bow and quickly fitted an arrow to it.

"I know the lad," said one of the yeomen "He is a minstrel. I saw him only a week ago. He was happy and gay then."

"Pah!" cried Stutely. "Wipe your eyes man. I do hate to see a tall, strong fellow sniveling like a girl of fourteen."

But Will Scarlet saw how the stranger, who had a young boyish face, was hurt by Stutely's words. Will Scarlet came to him and put his hand on the youth's shoulder.

"Do not mind these fellows," he said kindly. "They are rough, but they mean well. Perhaps they do not understand a lad like you. Come with us! We may be able to help you."

"Truly," said Will Stutely gruffly, "I mean no harm. We will be good to you. Take down your harp from the tree and come away with us into Sherwood Forest."

The youth walked beside Will Scarlet with

Will Scarlet Offers to Help the Youth.

a bowed head and sorrowful steps. Everything was still as the sun set, except for the forest's night sounds and the men's feet on the dry crisp leaves of last winter.

The little band moved across the glade. The air was filled with the sweet smell of good things cooking. Many yeomen turned and watched them as they arrived, but not one questioned them. With Will Scarlet on one side and Will Stutely on the other, the lad came to where Robin Hood sat with Little John standing beside him.

"Are you not the great Robin Hood?" he asked.

Robin was pleased that the lad knew of him, but frowned at Stutely when he learned that the lad had no money. Then Will Scarlet spoke up, saying the youth was in need.

Robin looked at the lad closely. "You have a young, kind face," he said, "a good face."

At Robin's kind words, the lad's eyes

144

Bringing the Youth to Robin

brimmed with tears. Robin sent the other men away, asking only Will Scarlet and Little John to stay. Then the lad explained his sadness.

"The girl I love, the fair Ellen, is to be married in two days to an old knight. She loves me, but it is her father's wish."

Robin quickly thought of a plan, but he needed a friar he could trust to help him. Will Scarlet said he knew a brave friar who lived only a half day's walk away. Robin planned to begin the journey at dawn.

The lad dried his eyes, and a merry feast was held. They asked him to sing for them.

Not a sound broke the stillness as the lad sang, so sweet was his voice and his music. Robin shook his hand and asked his name.

"Allan a Dale," came the reply. Then Will Scarlet gave his hand in fellowship, as did Little John. And so, the famous Allan a Dale became one of Robin Hood's band.

Allan a Dale Sings Sweetly.

Robin Dresses for an Adventure.

CHAPTER 13

Robin Seeks the Friar

Next morning, Robin put on a fine steel coat of chain mail and covered it with a jacket of Lincoln green. His steel cap was hidden by one of white leather with a cock's plume. The great bluish blade of his sword was marked all over with strange figures of dragons and winged women and whatnot.

Dressed this way, he and Little John, Will Scarlet, David of Doncaster, and Arthur a Bland set forth, leaving Will Stutely to be chief while Robin was gone.

They strode along, mile after mile. Will

Scarlet led, for he knew the way better than the others. In the hot silence of midday, they came to the banks of a wide, glassy stream. Swallows flew around them and over the water's surface, and gay dragonflies darted here and there, glistening in the sun.

"Now, good Uncle," said Will Scarlet after they had walked for a long time beside this sweet, bright river, "just beyond the bend before us is a shallow place to cross. On the other side of the stream lives the Friar of Fountain Dale."

Robin asked his yeomen to wait, for he wanted to go on this adventure alone. Little John grumbled at this, but the men sat down. Robin turned and left them.

He had walked just out of sight of his men when he stopped, for he thought he heard voices. Words seemed to pass between two men, but the voices were almost identical. Curious, Robin walked softly to the river

Robin Goes Off Alone.

bank, lay down on the grass, and peered over the edge.

All was cool and shady beneath the bank. There sat a friar with shoulders as broad as Little John's, merry gray eyes, and a curly black beard. He was eating a meat and onion pie and talking to himself, then answering himself as if he were another man.

Robin lay watching the friar. And when the friar began to sing, Robin joined in merrily. Then he leaped down the bank to where the friar sat.

"Do you know this country, good and holy man?" asked Robin, laughing.

"Yes, a bit," said the friar.

"Do you know a spot called Fountain Abbey?"

"Yes."

"Do you know the Friar of the Abbey?"

"Yes, a bit," came the answer.

Now Robin did not like the idea of getting

The Friar Talks to Himself.

his pretty clothes wet by crossing the river, so he asked the strong friar to take him across on his back.

At first, the man was angry, saying, "Do you dare ask me, the holy Tuck, to carry you?" But suddenly he paused. His eyes twinkled and he said he would carry Robin across.

When they reached the middle of the river where the water was deepest, the friar stopped. Then with a sudden lift of his hand and heave of his shoulders, he shot Robin over his head like a sack of grain and into the water with a mighty splash.

When Robin reached the bank again, their swords flashed in the sun and met with a clash that sounded far and near. They fought for over an hour, but neither man harmed the other.

"Hold!" shouted Robin, wiping the sweat from his brow. He thought it would be a ter-

Stopping in the Middle of the River

rible thing if he wounded this brave fellow or was wounded himself. "Will you let me blow on my bugle horn?" he asked.

The Friar nodded and watched for what Robin's call might bring. When he saw four tall men in Lincoln green, each with an arrow ready in his bow, he reached for a pretty silver whistle that hung with his rosary. He blew a loud, shrill blast, as a knight would to call a hawk, and four great shaggy hounds ran at Robin. Robin dropped his sword and leaped into a tree.

Then the hounds attacked the yeomen. All but Will Scarlet let their arrows fly. The dogs caught the arrows in their mouths and bit them in two. The men would certainly have been in trouble then if Will Scarlet had not stepped forth and called the dogs down. When they heard his voice, they licked his hands and barked.

"What is this?" cried the friar. "Do I see

The Friar Whistles for His Hounds.

young Master William Gamwell here with such men?"

"No, Friar Tuck," said the young man. "I am called Will Scarlet now, and this is my uncle, Robin Hood."

Robin jumped down from the tree. He was surprised to find that this friar was the friend of Scarlet's that he had been seeking. The friar was more surprised to find that Master William was one of the yeomen and that the man he had dropped in the river was Robin Hood.

"What do you need of me?" asked the friar.

"The day grows late," said Robin. "We cannot talk here. Come back with us to Sherwood, and I will tell you as we travel."

So they all departed with the dogs at their heels. It was long past nightfall before they reached the greenwood tree.

"Come Back with Us to Sherwood."

Waiting for the Wedding Party

CHAPTER 14

The Outlaws Go to Church

The day had come when fair Ellen was to be married, and Robin had sworn that she would marry only Allan a Dale. Robin had left Will Scarlet as chief and had taken Little John, Will Stutely, and several of his loyal men with him to the small church. He had dressed himself as a minstrel in red, yellow, and green. Ribbons and streamers hung all about him.

Now, he and his men were resting in the cool shadow of a wall after their long walk. He had sent David of Doncaster to watch the road from the top of the wall. After a time he asked, "Young David, what do you see?"

"I see white clouds and three black crows flying."

Silence fell again and time passed. Robin grew impatient and asked again. And David answered, "I see windmills swinging and poplar trees swaying."

So more time passed, till at last Robin asked young David once more what he saw, and David said, "I see how the wind makes waves in the barley field, and now over the hill comes an old friar to the church door."

Then Allan a Dale shook Friar Tuck who lay snoring by the wall. Robin knelt by Tuck and said, "Now go, and get yourself inside the church. Little John, Will Stutely, and I will follow you soon."

When Tuck had introduced himself to the old friar and been led inside the church, Robin took up his harp and sat beside the

David of Doncaster Keeps Watch.

door. Little John and Stutely took the bags of gold Robin had brought and went inside.

The wedding party came closer, and Robin could recognize them. The first was the rich Bishop of Hereford on a fine horse. Then came the Bishop's cousin, Sir Stephen—the groom, Ellen's stout father, and fair Ellen herself. She was pale and sad as she walked slowly into the church.

The Bishop stopped and asked Robin who he was.

"I am a harper," said Robin, "and I will play so sweetly this day that this fair bride will love the man she marries as long as they both live."

"If you do so," said the Bishop, "I will give you whatever you ask."

Robin smiled to himself. He planned to take some of the Bishop's money that day anyway, without the Bishop asking.

So he strode forward with his ribbons

A Harper Greets the Bishop.

fluttering and stopped the wedding. His men, led by a Allan a Dale, filled the church. Sir Stephen grew angry and insulted and left the church. When Robin offered Ellen's father the two bags of gold as a dowry, he could do little but accept it, for he realized that she would marry Allan with his consent or without it.

Then Friar Tuck stepped forward and gave Ellen's hand to Allan a Dale, who stood dizzy with happiness. The friar read the wedding service, and they were wed.

Robin had played his part and now asked the Bishop for the heavy golden chain he wore about his neck. The Bishop's cheeks grew red and his eyes flashed, but he handed Robin the chain. Robin flung it over Ellen's head so that it hung glittering on her shoulders.

"I thank you for your handsome gift," Robin said with a bow to the Bishop. "And if you are ever near Sherwood, I hope you will

Allan a Dale and Ellen Are Wed.

join us in a feast."

The Bishop scowled, for he knew what kind of feasts Robin Hood gave the rich in Sherwood.

Then Robin gathered his men together, with Allan and Ellen in their midst, and they all turned their footsteps toward the woodlands.

That night there was a greater and grander feast in Sherwood than there had ever been in all Nottinghamshire.

Friar Tuck asked Robin if he could join the band as their chaplain. Robin and the rest laughed. They knew that the friar loved his beer and the merry life, and they were pleased to have him. So Friar Tuck joined the band and lived for many days near the greenwood tree.

Friar Tuck Joins the Band.

Talking of Merry Days

CHAPTER 15

A Friar's Life and a Beggar's Life

Cold winter had passed and spring had come. Robin sat on a deer's hide in front of the greenwood tree with his hands clasped about his knees. He lazily watched as Little John rolled a bowstring from strands of hempen thread, wetting his palms and rolling the cord on his thigh. Nearby sat Allan a Dale, fitting a new string to his harp.

As Little John rubbed his new bowstring with yellow beeswax, he and Robin talked of the merry days they had spent at the Blue Boar Inn that past winter and of the many people they had met. They began wondering which of these people led the best life. Little John said that if he were not a yeoman, he would be a traveling friar. Friar Tuck sang a song in his rich, mellow voice, telling of the life of the traveling friar. He made it seem a good life, indeed. Robin said it was a good song, but he thought that beggars told merrier tales and led a merrier life.

"What do you say to an adventure this fair day, Little John?" suggested Robin. "Take a friar's gown from our chest of strange clothes, and I will stop the first beggar I meet and change clothes with him. Then we will wander the country and see what happens to each of us."

Little John agreed, and he went to the band's storehouse and chose a friar's robe for himself. When he came back, the rest of the men laughed at him for the robe was much too short. There was no beggar's costume in

The Robe Is Much Too Short.

the chest, so Robin took money to buy some beggar's clothes for himself.

Little John and Robin walked down the forest path until they came to the highway. They separated at the first fork, with Robin taking the road to Gainsborough and Little John, the road to Blyth.

"Farewell, holy father," called Robin, "and may you have no need to pray for your life before we meet again."

Little John answered, "Good day, beggar, and may you have no need to beg for mercy before I see you again."

That night in Sherwood, the red fires glowed brightly, making shadows in the trees and bushes. The brave fellows of the band lay around to hear Robin and Little John tell of their day's adventures.

First, Little John told of his meeting with three lasses, of their merry walk to market, and of the kiss he gave each lass when he left

Going on Separate Adventures

them. Then Robin told how he met a beggar under a lime tree and how he bought the man's clothes.

Next, Little John told of the tinker, the beggar, and the peddler who paid for all the ale he could drink at a small inn alongside the road. And Robin told of his adventure with four beggars: one who pretended to be deaf but had heard his steps, one who pretended to be blind but had seen him first, one who pretended he could not speak but had shouted a welcome, and one who pretended to be lame but had stood up and moved to let Robin sit down. Then he described the fight that began when the beggars found that he didn't know the secret words all beggars knew. It was a fight Robin had won, and he had the beggars' money to prove it.

Then, Little John told of the two Gray Friars who said they had no money to give him for food. Then he opened his hands and

Robin Meets Four Beggars.

showed the band the money the friars had in their pouches when he looked there.

Robin matched this story with one about the rich corn merchant who cheated the poor. Robin had told the merchant that he was dressed as a beggar to fool the thief, Robin Hood. The wicked merchant then told him that he hid all his money in his shoes for that very same reason. Robin ended his story by holding up the two shoes he had taken from the rich merchant.

Everyone listened closely to the stories, and the woods rang with laughter. Some thought the friar's life was best, and some thought the beggar's life was best.

The Rich Merchant's Shoes

The Queen's Page Rides to Sherwood.

CHAPTER 16

King Henry's Archery Match

The high road stretched white and dusty in the hot summer afternoon sun. Sixteen-year-old Richard Partington, the Queen's page, rode along on a milk-white horse, and his long cloak flowed behind him. He wore silk and velvet, with jewels flashing and a dagger jingling against the front of his saddle.

He had been riding since dawn on the hot, dusty road and was pleased to come to the cool shady inn bearing the sign of a Blue Boar.

Five men sat drinking ale under a large oak tree. Two were dressed in Lincoln green. One was the tallest, stoutest man Partington had ever seen. The other was a handsome fellow with a sunburnt face and curly nut-brown hair.

The innkeeper brought the page his wine and handed it up to him. From his saddle, Partington toasted Queen Eleanor and Robin Hood, whom he was seeking.

Hearing this, two of the yeomen whispered to each other. Then the tall one said, "Surely it is safe to take him to Robin, Will."

In the cool shade of the greenwood tree, Robin and many of the band lay on the soft green grass and listened while Allan a Dale sang and played upon his sweet-sounding harp. There came a sudden sound of horses' feet. Little John and Will Stutely came riding in with young Richard Partington between them. Robin stood to meet him, and young

"It Is Safe to Take Him to Robin."

Partington leaped from his horse, taking with him a small velvet box.

"Welcome!" cried Robin. "What brings one in such noble dress to our poor forest of Sherwood?"

Young Partington told them of King Henry's grand shooting match in London Town and of the Queen's wish that Robin come and take the prize. She had sent a golden ring from her thumb as a token of her good will and her promise that Robin would be protected from arrest if he came.

Robin Hood kissed the ring and slipped it on his little finger. "I will do our Queen's bidding and go with you to London."

"We have no time to waste," said the page "We have only four days to make our long journey."

"I will choose three men to go with me," said Robin. "Little John, my right-hand man, Will Scarlet, my cousin, and Allan a Dale, my

Robin Kisses the Queen's Ring.

minstrel. Will Stutely shall be chief while I am gone."

They were a fine sight as they rode into London Town. Robin was dressed in blue, Little John and Will Scarlet were in Lincoln green, and Allan a Dale was in scarlet from the top of his head to his pointed shoes. Each man wore a headcap of polished steel and a coat of linked mail under his jerkin.

Robin Hood, Little John, Will Scarlet, and Allan a Dale kneeled before the Queen in the royal garden room. Great floods of golden sunshine poured in through the windows, and the air smelled of sweet red roses from the beautiful garden below.

After a rich feast, the Queen asked them to tell of their adventures. They told her every story they could remember, and the Queen and her ladies in waiting laughed again and again. Then Allan sang for them, and so the time passed till the hour of the great archery

Kneeling Before the Queen

match.

Bright flags fluttered in the breeze for each band of royal archers, and silken streamers of red, white, green, and blue hung from the crowded galleries.

Six trumpeters entered the field. Velvet banners worked in silver and gold threads hung from their silver trumpets. Behind them came King Henry and Queen Eleanor. Then came the court, and the field was full of color.

The Queen made a bet with the King. She said she knew three archers who could out-shoot the King's best men. The crowd stood to see who the men could be. No one knew the men, but the Bishop of Hereford, who stood by the Queen, gasped. Even though Robin called himself Locksley, after the town where he was born, the Bishop recognized him.

There were eight hundred archers in all. So many arrows were shot that the targets

The Bishop Recognizes Robin.

looked like porcupines. Even with a rematch, no man could outshoot Locksley and the two men in Lincoln green.

When the tournament was over, the yeomen of the King's guard and many of the crowd gathered around the strangers. While Robin was talking to Gilbert, the King's best archer, another plucked him by the sleeve and said, "Richard Partington sends this message from a certain lady, 'The lion growls. Beware of your head.'"

Robin knew the message came from the Queen and meant the King was angry. It was now dangerous for them to stay. He called his three yomen together. Without further delay, they pushed through the crowd and left London, heading northward.

"Beware of Your Head."

Four Shadows Walk the Road.

CHAPTER 17

Robin Escapes Capture

The great moon floated in the sky. The four fellows walked the road like four shadows. They came to an inn, and Robin suggested they stay the night.

"We are still very near London, Uncle," said Will Scarlet.

Nevertheless, they entered the inn. As they ate, Little John winked at the young lass who served them.

During the meal, the landlord came to the table and said that Richard Partington wished to see the lad in blue. Robin rose quickly and went outside.

"The Bishop of Hereford has turned the King against you," said Partington. "The King sent men to arrest you at the archery fields, but you had gone. Now, he has one thousand men on this road to take you. The Bishop leads them, and he has sworn to hang you. The Queen sent me to warn you."

"I will go one way tonight and send my friends another way," said Robin. "And I will let the landlord think we are all going to St. Albans. You have saved my life again, Richard Partington. I will not forget it."

"Farewell, sir," said young Partington. "Go safely." The two shook hands, and the lad turned his horse back to London.

The yeomen left the inn. "Now," said Robin, "be sly. Will Scarlet, you shall lead." Then Robin shook hands with his three friends, and they parted.

Not long after this, twenty of the King's

"The Bishop Has Sworn to Hang You."

men rode to the door of the inn. The innkeeper told the King's men that Robin Hood and his men were riding to St. Albans.

Will Scarlet, Allan a Dale, and Little John reached Sherwood in eight days with no trouble from the King's men. But Robin was not at the greenwood tree when they arrived. He had not been as lucky as they.

When the Bishop found he had been tricked at St. Albans, he took all his men and blocked every road into Sherwood. The Sheriff of Nottingham joined the army. By this time, the three yeomen were safe, but Robin was still a day's journey from Sherwood, unaware of the danger all around him.

As he knelt by a stream drinking from his cupped hands, something hissed past his ear and splashed into the water beside him. Quick as a wink, Robin sprang to his feet, crossed the stream, and plunged into the thicket. He knew it was an arrow that had

Danger All Around!

passed his head, and he would be dead if he did not run.

Six more arrows rattled after him, and one would have wounded him badly, but it struck his coat of steel. Seven men came after him, but Robin knew the ground better than they, and he soon left them far behind.

He had gone a mile when he saw another band of the King's men over a hill. Before they could see him, he turned and ran back the way he had come. He ran mile after mile until he could run no more.

As Robin rested in a hedge, Quince the Cobbler came by. Robin offered to trade his own fine blue clothes for Quince's rough, patched jerkin. Quince thought this was a merry idea, even when the King's men found him and arrested him because they thought he was Robin Hood.

Robin was so tired he couldn't walk any farther. A storm was coming, and he decided

The King's Men Come After Robin.

to spend the night in an inn. Rooms were shared in small inns, and when Robin awoke the next morning, he found a friar snoring next to him. He put on the friar's gown and left the inn.

In the afternoon, Robin met Sir Richard of Lea, a knight he had helped some years before when Sir Richard had tried to visit Sherwood, but was turned away.

The Sheriff's men were now in front of Robin, the King's men were behind him, and they knew of his disguise. Robin's heart sank, for he had no place to hide.

Sir Richard offered to help. He took Robin to his castle, disguised him as one of his men, and brought him to Queen Eleanor to ask for her protection.

The Queen was indeed surprised when Robin dropped lightly to the ground inside the garden wall. But she went directly to the King and pleaded for his life.

Robin Surprises the Queen.

Sir Robert, a friend of the Queen's, came to Robin and said, "If it were not for the Queen, you would be a dead man. Let this danger teach you two lessons: first, be more honest, and second, be less bold in your comings and goings, or someday a trap will catch you. You have put your head in the angry lion's mouth and escaped. Do not try it again."

The Queen returned with Edward Cunningham, the King's head page, and announced that the page would take Robin safely back to Sherwood and see that no harm came to him.

Three days later, they set out. They passed many of the King's men returning to London, but none of them stopped the two travelers. It was the Queen who had saved Robin.

Robin followed Sir Robert's advice and never went so far from Sherwood that he could not return easily and quickly.

Riding Safely out of London

Robin Wakes Little John.

CHAPTER 18

The Evil Guy of Gisbourne

A long time passed after the great shooting match, and much happened. King Henry died, and King Richard came to the throne with adventures as daring as those of Robin Hood. But none of these changes reached quiet Sherwood Forest, and the band lived as they always had.

One summer day, the birds' singing wakened Robin. He woke Little John, and the two set off for an adventure. Little John took the road to the left, Robin took the path to the right.

Now the Bishop of Hereford and the Sheriff had hired the evil Guy of Gisbourne, a murderer and a thief, to capture Robin Hood, dead or alive. They promised a full pardon and two hundred pounds reward to this man who said he would kill his own brother for such money.

Guy of Gisbourne wore a horse's hide with the hair still on it. On his head and over his face he wore a horsehide hood with ears that stuck up like rabbit's ears. He carried a huge sword, sharpened on both edges, a yew bow, and a dagger.

Robin came upon this black-hearted man suddenly as he walked along. Guy of Gibourne glared at him wickedly. He pushed back his hood and showed his fierce black eyes, hooked nose, and thin cruel mouth.

Robin returned his gaze without a smile. "You bloody villain!" he cried fiercely. "Look at daylight for the last time."

The Evil Guy of Gisbourne

Each man knew that either he or the other must die. There would be no mercy shown.

Their swords flashed. Soon the grass was trampled by their feet and sprinkled with Guy of Gisbourne's blood. At last, Guy made a deadly stab at Robin. Robin stepped back lightly, but caught his heel in a root and fell heavily on his back. With a grin Guy stabbed at Robin, but Robin caught the blade in his hand and pushed it aside. It cut into his palm, but gave him time to leap up and stab Guy below the sword arm and kill him.

Robin wiped his sword and talked softly to himself. "I am sorry I killed the forester when I was a youth, but I am glad I have killed you, Guy of Gisbourne."

Then he put on Guy's hairy garment, bloody as it was, and picked up the other's sword and bow with his own. He pulled the hood over his face and set off to take revenge on the Sheriff. Many hid away from him as

Robin Falls on His Back.

he walked, for all were terrified by Guy of Gisbourne.

Meanwhile, Little John had been taken prisoner by the Sheriff and was now awaiting death by the hanging tree. This is how it happened.

Little John had met an old woman who was weeping bitterly, for the Sheriff had taken her three sons to hang for killing a deer. Little John had a tender heart for the sorrows of others and wanted to help her. When she told him that the Sheriff was only waiting for the return of the man he had sent after Robin Hood, Little John hurried to disguise himself. Then, dressed as a friar, he went quickly to find the Sheriff, for now he feared for Robin's life as well.

He came to the oak tree where the three youths stood. The nooses were already around their necks. Little John asked if he could step up and hear the youths' confessions before

Little John Helps an Old Woman.

they were hung. His hair and beard were white, and he walked and talked like an old man. The Sheriff looked hard at him, but did not recognize him.

Little John went to the lads and whispered in their ears, while slyly cutting their bonds. The Sheriff and his men took no notice as Little John fitted an arrow to his bowstring.

"Run!" shouted Little John in a mighty voice.

The youths flung the nooses from their necks and sped into the forest. Little John raised his deadly bow, but as he drew the arrow back, the bow split. Then the Sheriff rode down on him and knocked him senseless.

When he opened his eyes, his hands and legs were bound. He was dazed from the blow and sat leaning against the hanging tree. As he looked around him, his heart crumbled. For before him stood the evil Guy of

Bound at the Hanging Tree

Gisbourne, his clothes covered with blood and Robin's bugle horn and bow in his hand. Tears rolled down Little John's brown cheeks, and he thought it would be good to die since Robin had also been slain.

But the Sheriff clapped his hands for joy. Guy said he wanted to kill Little John as a reward, and he stepped boldly up to the huge man.

"Peace, Little John!" whispered Robin. "Could you not tell it was me under this hide?" And he cut him free, threw back his hood, and blew three loud blasts on his horn.

When the Sheriff saw this, he thought Robin was the devil himself. Neither he nor his men were brave enough to face Robin Hood and Little John when they were armed, so they turned their horses and fled.

When Will Stutely and a dozen stout yeomen arrived, they found Robin and Little John alone and glad to be alive.

Robin Cuts Little John Free.

King Richard's Procession

CHAPTER 19

King Richard Comes to Sherwood

Two months later, all Nottinghamshire was in a stir, for King Richard was coming to visit the Sheriff. The stony streets, decorated with colorful banners, were full of townspeople and countryfolk. The King's procession rode into town with trumpeters and knights in armor, pages in silk and velvet, and men-at-arms. The King rode alongside the Sheriff. He was a head taller, with golden hair and beard and eyes as blue as the sky. He wore a broad, heavy chain about his neck.

Robin, Friar Tuck, Little John, Will Scarlet, Allan a Dale, Will Stutely, and others of the band were in the crowd that day, cheering the King. They loved him loyally because his deeds were so like their own.

At the great feast in the Guild Hall, the King asked the Sheriff to tell him of Robin Hood. Both the Sheriff and the Bishop of Hereford were silent.

Then young Henry of Lea, a favorite with the King, told the story of how Robin had once used the Bishop's money to help Sir Richard of Lea, his father. Soon, others were telling tales of Robin's adventures.

That night, the King's mind was still on Robin. Sir Hubert of Bingham laughed and said, "It would not be so hard to meet the fellow, Your Majesty. If we dress as friars and carry full purses, no doubt we will meet and dine with him in Sherwood before the day is over."

The King was pleased with the plan and set out early the next morning with seven of

The King Hears Tales of Robin Hood.

his men. Later in the day, when they were well within the forest, the King said, "I would give fifty pounds for something to drink now."

Just as he spoke, a tall fellow with yellow hair and beard and merry blue eyes stepped out from the bushes and grabbed the King's bridle rein.

"I must answer such a request, holy brother," said Robin. "We keep an inn nearby and, for fifty pounds, we will give you a noble feast." He gave a shrill whistle, and sixty men joined him.

"There is no need for force," said the King sternly. "Here is my purse."

"Hut, tut!" said Robin. "What proud words! Are you the King of England to speak so? Here, Will, take this purse."

Will Scarlet took the purse and counted the money. Robin told him to keep half of it and return the rest. When he asked the King

Robbing the "Friars" of Their Purses

to take off his hood, the King said he kept it on for religious reasons, and Robin pressed him no further.

Little John had also taken sixty yeomen to bring back a rich guest, but had not yet returned. Friar Tuck sat with forty strong men under the greenwood tree. Tuck welcomed the new "friars," and they all drank to the health of King Richard, even the King, himself.

Then it was time for sport. A target was set with a mark four fingers wide. Any archer who missed the mark received a punch from Will Scarlet's fist.

First David of Doncaster shot, and shot well. Next, Midge the Miller, and then Wat the Tinker. All the band shot, some getting off free and some getting a punch that left them on the grass.

The King watched Robin closely, hoping to persuade him to join his guards. It was

Drinking to the Health of the King

Robin's turn, but his last arrow was feathered badly, and it missed the mark. Robin threw his bow to the ground in anger, and the band roared with laughter.

"Come, Uncle," said Will Scarlet in his soft voice, "I have something for you."

"No!" said Robin. "I will take my beating from the tall friar instead of from you, Will. And if the friar knocks me to the grass, I will return his money."

King Richard tumbled Robin to the ground, and Will Scarlet was counting out his money when Little John burst into the glade with Richard of Lea and sixty yeomen.

"Gather your band and come with me," shouted Sir Richard of Lea. "The King is coming to the forest for you. Come to Castle Lea until this danger is past."

Then his face suddenly grew pale, and he kneeled before the tall friar, for he recognized him as the King.

Kneeling Before the King

King Richard removed his hood, and all knelt before him.

The King scolded Sir Richard for helping an outlaw hide, but softened when the knight and his son, Sir Henry of Lea, boldly stood by Robin as he had stood by them once.

This was the last day Robin Hood spent in Sherwood for many years, for the King ordered Robin and his nephew, Will Scarlet, Little John and Allan a Dale, his minstrel, to become part of his household in London Town. A full pardon was given to each man, and the band became royal rangers.

After a year or two at court, Little John came back to Nottingham and lived near the forest. Will Scarlet returned to his home. Robin was made Earl of Huntingdon and followed the King to many wars. Allan a Dale and fair Ellen lived at court with Robin for all the years he served the King.

But Robin Hood did return to Sherwood for one last great bout.

Robin Leaves Sherwood.

Returning to Sherwood Years Later

CHAPTER 20

Robin Hood's Death

King Richard died bravely on the battle-field, a lion-hearted king. After a time, the Earl of Huntingdon, or Robin Hood as we call him, had a great longing to see his woodlands again. King John, who succeeded King Richard, let Robin go, but asked that he stay only three days in Sherwood.

Robin and Allan a Dale left that same day, and as they traveled, they talked of old, familiar things.

"Look, Allan!" cried Robin. "See the scar on that tree? That was the day your arrow missed a deer and stripped away a piece of bark instead. And we got caught in a storm and stayed in the old farmer's hut." Robin seemed to remember every stick and stone, every path he had walked with Little John, every tree he had used as a target.

At last, they came to the open glade and the greenwood tree. Neither man spoke. Robin looked about him. All was the same, yet so different, for the many busy fellows that had filled the glade were gone, and all was still. Robin's eyes filled with tears. He had his bugle horn over his shoulder, and now he raised it to his lips.

"Tirilia, lirila," the notes went down the forest paths, echoing until they faded away and were lost.

Now Little John, who still lived near the forest, was out walking, deep in thought, when he heard the faint notes of a distant horn. He gave a great cry and ran straight

Tearfully Remembering Familiar Things

through the trees. He ran and ran until he came to the glade. When he saw Robin, he hugged him so hard, he picked him up off the ground.

In a shower of snapping twigs, seven royal rangers burst from the bushes with Will Stutely at their head. Then two more came, with Will Scathelock and Midge the Miller.

Robin looked about and said, "I swear I will never leave these woodlands again. I will forget Robert, Earl of Huntingdon, and be Robin Hood once more."

King John was furious. He sent Sir William Dale and the Sheriff of Nottingham to capture Robin, dead or alive. The Sheriff died in the bloody battle, and Sir William was wounded, but Robin was not captured. However, he brooded so long over the deaths of many of his men that he came down with a fever.

Men thought fevers could be cured by

Little John Welcomes Robin.

taking a bit of blood, so Robin rode with Little John to his cousin, the Prioress of the nunnery in Kirlees, who was skilled at blood-letting.

The Prioress feared that the King would be angry if she helped Robin, so she locked Little John out of the nunnery and led Robin up a winding stone stair to a room in a high tower. There, she tied a cord around her cousin's arm as if to bleed him. But instead, she cut a vein and then left him, locking the door behind her. Again and again Robin called for help, but no one came. His cousin had betrayed him! And Little John couldn't hear him.

Robin bled and bled until he felt his strength slip away. He stood up weakly and leaned against the wall to reach his bugle. He blew three faint notes. Still, Little John heard them in the glade where he lay.

Little John was mad with grief and fear.

The Prioress Leads Robin to the Tower.

He lifted a huge stone post and rammed it at the bolted nunnery door. The door crashed open, and the frightened nuns ran away. Little John raced to the tower and forced the door open with his shoulder. He burst in and saw Robin, his face white and drawn, leaning against the gray stone wall.

Little John picked him up and gently laid him on the bed. Then he applied some bandages to stop the bleeding. He lifted Robin against his own strong shoulder so that he could see the woodlands through the window. He tried to cheer Robin, but Robin took Little John's rough brown fist in his white hands and said, "Dear friend, we will never walk in the forest together again."

Little John was silent. Hot tears fell from his eyes.

Robin chokingly asked Little John to string his bow and fit a smooth arrow for him. "Little John, my friend, watch this arrow as I

Little John Rams the Bolted Door.

shoot and dig my grave on the spot where it lands."

And the last of Robin's strength flew from his body as the arrow sped from the bow.

So died Robin Hood in the year 1247.

Loud, sorrowful cries rose from the dark shadows of Sherwood Forest, but Robin Hood's yeomen lived long after him and handed down these tales of his brave deeds to their children. And these children handed them down to their children and to their children's children.

"Dig My Grave on the Spot Where It Lands."